The Man From Missouri   Harry S. Truman

The Memorable
Words
of the
Thirty-Third
President

Harry S. Truman

Selected
and Arranged by
Ted Sheldon
Illustrated
With Photographs
From the
Harry S. Truman
Library

The Man

From

Missouri

♛ Hallmark Editions

Contents

Peace

Harry S. Truman was President of the United States during two major wars—World War II and the Korean Conflict. Perhaps due to the awesome burdens he bore during these two periods, Truman spoke often and eloquently of global peace. In 1943, when Truman was a U.S. Senator from Missouri, he spoke these words on the floor of the Senate, urging a major financial commitment to global peace as soon as World War II— then raging—was over:

I am just as sure as I can be that this World War is the result of the 1919-20 isolationist attitude, and I am equally sure that another and a worse war will follow this one, unless the United Nations and their allies, and all the other sovereign nations decide to work together for peace as they are working together for victory.

I want this greatest of legislative bodies to go on record in no uncertain terms that it will not again contribute to a condition that will cause another world war.

In a radio broadcast in April, 1945, on the occasion of the founding of the United Nations:

We can no longer permit any nation, or group of nations, to attempt to settle their arguments with bombs and bayonets.

If we continue to abide by such decisions, we will be forced to accept the fundamental philosophy of our enemies, namely, that "Might Makes Right." To deny this premise, and we most certainly do, we are obliged to provide the necessary means to refute it. Words are not enough.

We must, once and for all, reverse the order, and prove by our acts conclusively, that Right Has Might.

If we do not want to die together in war, we must learn to live together in peace.

From President Truman's REPORT TO THE NATION *on network radio, following the surrender of Nazi Germany in 1945:*

Our victory in Europe was more than a victory of arms. It was a victory of one way of life over another. It was a victory of an ideal founded on the rights of the common man, on the dignity of the human being, and on the conception of the State as the servant—not the master—of its people.

A free people showed that it was able to defeat professional soldiers whose only moral arms were obedience and worship of force.

We tell ourselves that we have emerged from this war the most powerful nation in the world—the most powerful nation, perhaps, in all history. That is true, but not in the sense some of us believe it to be true.

The war has shown us that we have tremendous resources to make all the materials for war. It has shown us that we have skillful workers and managers and able generals, and a brave people capable of bearing arms.

All these things we knew before.

The new thing—the thing we had not known—the thing we have learned now and should never forget, is this: that a society of self-governing men is more powerful, more enduring, more creative than any other kind of society, however disciplined, however centralized.

We know now that the basic proposition of the worth and dignity of man is not a sentimental aspiration or a vain hope or a piece of rhetoric. It is the strongest, the most creative force now present in this world.

Now let us use that force and all our resources and all our skills in the great cause of a just and lasting peace!

On August 9, 1945, the United States dropped an atomic bomb on Nagasaki. That same day, President Truman felt compelled to explain to "all peace-loving nations" of the world why he had made the fateful decision—in the name of peace—to use the most powerful weapon of war then known to man. In Truman's words:

I realize the tragic significance of the atomic bomb.

Its production and its use were not lightly undertaken by this Government. But we knew that our enemies were on the search for it. We know now how close they were to finding it. And we knew the disaster which would come to this Nation, and to all peace-loving nations, to all civilization, if they had found it first.

That is why we felt compelled to undertake the long and uncertain and costly labor of its discovery and production.

We won the race of discovery against the Germans.

Having found the bomb we have used it. We have used it against those who attacked us without warning at Pearl Harbor, against those who have starved and beaten and executed American prisoners of war, against those who have abandoned all pretense of obeying international laws of warfare. We have used it in order to shorten the agony of war, in order to save the lives of thousands and thousands of Americans.

We shall continue to use it until we completely destroy Japan's power to make war. Only a Japanese surrender will stop us.

In February, 1948, at the height of the Cold War between the United States and the Soviet Union, a Communist coup d'etat in Czechoslovakia shocked the world and chilled American hopes for a peaceful coexistence. President Truman requested immediate reenactment of the military draft system, which had been dropped after World War II, in order to increase the nation's armed forces to a level he believed necessary to deter any further Communist aggression. On March 17, 1948, the President addressed a joint session of Congress:

Until the free nations of Europe have regained their strength, and so long as Communism threatens the very existence of democracy, the United States must remain strong enough to support those countries of Europe which are threatened with Communist control and police-state rule. . . .

I recommend the temporary reenactment of selective-service legislation in order to maintain our armed forces at their authorized strength. . . .

We cannot meet our international responsibilities unless we maintain our armed forces. It is of vital importance, for example, that we keep our occupation forces in Germany until the peace is secure. . . .

We must be prepared to pay the price of peace, or assuredly we shall pay the price of war.

We in the United States remain determined to seek, by every possible means, a just and honorable basis for the settlement of international issues. We shall continue to give our strong allegiance to the United Nations as the principal means for international security based on law, not on force. We shall remain ready and anxious to join with all nations—I repeat, with *all* nations—in every possible effort to reach international understanding and agreement.

The door has never been closed, nor will it ever be closed, to the Soviet Union or any other nation which will genuinely cooperate in preserving the peace.

At the same time, we must not be confused about the central issue which confronts the world today.

The time has come when the free men and women of the world must face the threat to their liberty squarely and courageously.

The United States has a tremendous responsibility to act according to the measure of our power for good in the world. We have learned that we must earn the peace we seek just as we earned victory in war, not by wishful thinking, but by realistic effort.

At no time in our history has unity among our people been so vital as it is at the present time.

Unity of purpose, unity of effort, and unity of spirit are essential to accomplish the task before us. . . .

In an address to the Chiefs of Mission of the Marshall Plan countries in 1949, Truman expressed his "great hope for peace and prosperity":

It is not new for nations to fight together against a common enemy. But it is new for nations to work together, as our nations are working together now, in close economic cooperation to create a better life for their citizens and to build a lasting peace.

I believe that, in years to come, we shall look back upon this undertaking as the dividing line between the old era of world affairs and the new—the dividing line between the old era of national suspicion, economic hostility, and isolationism, and the new era of mutual cooperation to increase the prosperity of people throughout the world....

Our great hope for peace and prosperity lies in the developing sense of unity among the free nations of the world. We have learned full well that no nation can live to itself alone. And we have also learned that when the free peoples of the world stand united they are unconquerable.

The United States will continue to dedicate its strength and resources to the building of a peaceful and prosperous world.

On April 10, 1951, President Truman relieved General Douglas MacArthur of his command of U.S. forces in Korea. The reason was straightforward: MacArthur had insisted that the United States strike at China because China was supplying troops and weapons to North Korea. Truman said no. When MacArthur refused to accept the decision of the President, who was his Commander-in-Chief, the President removed him from command. The following day, Truman explained his action to the nation. His radio address that day went far beyond the question of MacArthur's proposed strategy in Korea:

I want to talk plainly to you tonight about what we are doing in Korea and about our policy in the Far East.

In the simplest terms, what we are doing in Korea is this: We are trying to prevent a third world war.

I think most people in this country recognized that fact last June. And they warmly supported the decision of the Government to help the Republic of Korea against the Communist aggressors. Now, many persons, even some who applauded our decision to defend Korea, have forgotten the basic reason for our action.

It is right for us to be in Korea. It was right last June. It is right today.

I want to remind you why this is true.

The Communists in the Kremlin are engaged in a monstrous conspiracy to stamp out freedom all over the world. If they were to succeed, the United States would be numbered among their principal victims. It must be clear to everyone that the United States can-not—and will not—sit idly by and await foreign con-quest. The only question is: When is the best time to meet the threat and how is the best way to meet it?

The best time to meet the threat is in the beginning. It is easier to put out a fire in the beginning when it is small than after it has become a roaring blaze.

And the best way to meet the threat of aggression is for the peace-loving nations to act together. If they don't act together, they are likely to be picked off one by one.

If they had followed the right policies in the 1930's —if the free countries had acted together, to crush the aggression of the dictators, and if they had acted in the beginning, when the aggression was small—there probably would have been no World War II.

If history has taught us anything, it is that aggres-sion anywhere in the world is a threat to peace every-where in the world. . . .

So far, we have prevented World War III.

So far, by fighting a limited war in Korea, we have prevented aggression from succeeding, and bringing on a general war. And the ability of the whole free world to resist Communist aggression has been greatly improved. . . .

We do not want to see the conflict in Korea ex-tended. We are trying to prevent a world war—not to start one. The best way to do that is to make it plain that we and the other free countries will continue to resist the attack. . . .

But you may ask why can't we take other steps to punish the aggressor. Why don't we bomb Manchuria and China itself? Why don't we assist Chinese Nationalist troops to land on the mainland of China?

If we were to do these things, [we] would be running a very grave risk of starting a general war. If that were to happen, we would have brought about the exact situation we are trying to prevent.

If we were to do these things, we would become entangled in a vast conflict on the continent of Asia and our task would become immeasurably more difficult all over the world.

What would suit the ambitions of the Kremlin better than for our military forces to be committed to a full scale war with Red China?

It may well be that, in spite of our best efforts, the Communists may spread the war. But it would be wrong—tragically wrong—for us to take the initiative in extending the war.

The dangers are great. Make no mistake about it. Behind the North Koreans and Chinese Communists in the front lines stand additional millions of Chinese soldiers. And behind the Chinese stand the tanks, the planes, the submarines, the soldiers, and the scheming rulers of the Soviet Union.

Our aim is to avoid the spread of the conflict.

Brothers Vivian and Harry S. Truman, ages 2 and 4. Notice the future President's cane.

Young Harry Truman in his Battery 'B' uniform on his father's farm in 1911.

Lieutenant Harry S. Truman of the 129th Field Artillery during World War I.

Senator and Mrs. Truman at the 1944 Convention, where the Senator received his surprise nomination.

President Franklin Delano Roosevelt with his Vice President, Harry Truman.

*nounced it as "socialized medicine"; his own descrip-
tion follows:*

Millions of our citizens do not now have a full measure or opportunity to achieve and enjoy good health. Millions do not now have protection or security against the economic effects of sickness. The time has arrived for action to help them attain that opportunity and that protection. . . .

People with low or moderate incomes do not get the same medical attention as those with high incomes. The poor have more sickness, but they get less medical care. People who live in rural areas do not get the same amount or quality of medical attention as those who live in our cities. . . . The principal reason why people do not receive the care they need is that they cannot afford to pay for it on an individual basis at the time they need it. This is true not only for needy persons. It is also true for a large proportion of normally self-supporting persons. . . .

Everyone should have ready access to all necessary medical, hospital and related services.

I recommend solving the basic problem by distributing the costs through expansion of our existing compulsory social insurance system. This is not socialized medicine.

Everyone who carries fire insurance knows how the law of averages is made to work so as to spread the risk, and to benefit the insured who actually suffers

Senator and Mrs. Truman at the 1944 Convention, where the Senator received his surprise nomination.

President Franklin Delano Roosevelt with his Vice President, Harry Truman.

President Truman and his family attend funeral services for the late President Roosevelt at Hyde Park.

Democracy

Truman's concept of democracy embraced a view of human cooperation for human betterment that was almost reverential. In his first State of the Union Address, he turned his attentions to the future: "We face a great peacetime venture; the challenging venture of a free enterprise economy making full and effective use of its rich resources and technical advances. This is a venture in which business, agriculture, and labor have vastly greater opportunities than heretofore. But they all also have vastly greater responsibilities." He believed that a democratic people, supporting a just cause, could literally change the world. One of his most bitter disappointments was the nation's refusal to support, through their elected representatives, his proposals for a comprehensive medical care program. First presented in 1945, the heart of his program was compulsory national health insurance. His critics de-

nounced it as "socialized medicine"; his own descrip-
tion follows:

Millions of our citizens do not now have a full
measure or opportunity to achieve and enjoy good
health. Millions do not now have protection or security against the economic effects of sickness. The time
has arrived for action to help them attain that opportunity and that protection. . . .

People with low or moderate incomes do not get the
same medical attention as those with high incomes.
The poor have more sickness, but they get less medical
care. People who live in rural areas do not get the same
amount or quality of medical attention as those who
live in our cities. . . . The principal reason why people
do not receive the care they need is that they cannot
afford to pay for it on an individual basis at the time
they need it. This is true not only for needy persons. It
is also true for a large proportion of normally self-
supporting persons. . . .

Everyone should have ready access to all necessary
medical, hospital and related services.

I recommend solving the basic problem by distributing the costs through expansion of our existing compulsory social insurance system. This is not socialized
medicine.

Everyone who carries fire insurance knows how the
law of averages is made to work so as to spread the
risk, and to benefit the insured who actually suffers

the loss. If instead of the costs of sickness being paid only by those who get sick, all the people—sick and well—were required to pay premiums into an insurance fund, the pool of funds thus created would enable all who do fall sick to be adequately served without overburdening anyone. That is the principle upon which all forms of insurance are based.

People should remain free to choose their own physicians and hospitals. The removal of financial barriers between patient and doctor would enlarge the present freedom of choice. The legal requirement on the population to contribute involves no compulsion over the doctor's freedom to decide what services his patient needs. People will remain free to obtain and pay for medical service outside the health insurance system if they desire, even though they are members of the system; just as they are free to send their children to private instead of to public schools, although they must pay taxes for public schools. . . .

None of this is really new. The American people are the most insurance-minded people in the world. They will not be frightened off from health insurance because some people have misnamed it "socialized medicine."

I repeat—what I am recommending is not socialized medicine.

Socialized medicine means that all doctors work as employees of government. The American people want no such system. No such system is here proposed.

Under the plan I suggest, our people would continue to get medical and hospital services just as they do now—on the basis of their own voluntary decisions and choices. Our doctors and hospitals would continue to deal with disease with the same professional freedom as now. There would, however, be this all-important difference: whether or not patients get the services they need would not depend on how much they can afford to pay at the time.

I am in favor of the broadest possible coverage for this insurance system....

We are a rich nation and can afford many things. But ill-health which can be prevented or cured is one thing we cannot afford.

The ideal of democracy figured largely in the President's State of the Union Address in 1948. He turned his attention to those goals that directly related to "the foundations of our democracy and the happiness of our people":

It was ten years ago that the determination of dictators to wage war upon mankind became apparent. The years that followed brought untold death and destruction.

We shared in the human suffering of the war, but we were fortunate enough to escape most of war's destruction. We were able through these ten years to expand the productive strength of our farms and factories. More important, however, is the fact that these years brought us new courage and new confidence in the ideals of our free democracy. Our deep belief in freedom and justice was reinforced in the crucible of war.

On the foundations of our greatly strengthened economy and our renewed confidence in democratic values we can continue to move forward. ·

There are some who look with fear and distrust upon planning for the future; yet our great national achievements have been attained by those with vision. Our Union was formed, our frontiers were pushed back, and our great industries were built by men who looked ahead.

I propose that we look ahead today toward those goals for the future which have the greatest bearing upon the foundations of our democracy and the happiness of our people.

I do so, confident in the thought that with clear objectives and with firm determination we can, in the next ten years, build upon the accomplishments of the past decade to achieve a glorious future. Year by year, beginning now, we must make a substantial part of this progress.

Our goal is to secure fully the essential human rights of our citizens.

The United States has always had a deep concern for human rights. Religious freedom, free speech, and freedom of thought are cherished realities in our land. Any denial of human rights is a denial of the basic beliefs of democracy and of our regard for the worth of each individual.

Today, however, some of our citizens are still denied equal opportunity for education, for jobs and economic advancement, and for the expression of their views at the polls. Most serious of all, some are denied equal protection under our laws. Whether discrimination is based on race, or creed, or color, or land of origin, it is utterly contrary to American ideals of democracy.

In his Inaugural Address, in 1949, he delivered a ringing speech on democracy:

Communism is based on the belief that man is so weak and inadequate that he is unable to govern himself, and therefore requires the rule of strong masters.

Democracy is based on the conviction that man has the moral and intellectual capacity, as well as the inalienable right, to govern himself with reason and justice.

Communism subjects the individual to arrest without lawful cause, punishment without trial, and forced labor as the chattel of the state. It decrees what information he shall receive, what art he shall produce, what leaders he shall follow, and what thoughts he shall think.

Democracy maintains that government is established for the benefit of the individual, and is charged with the responsibility of protecting the rights of the individual and his freedom in the exercise of his abilities.

Communism maintains that social wrongs can be corrected only by violence.

Democracy has proved that social justice can be achieved through peaceful change.

Communism holds that the world is so deeply divided into opposing classes that war is inevitable.

Democracy holds that free nations can settle differences justly and maintain lasting peace.

These differences between communism and democracy do not concern the United States alone. People everywhere are coming to realize that what is involved is material well-being, human dignity, and the right to believe in and worship God.

I state these differences, not to draw issues of belief as such, but because the actions resulting from the Communist philosophy are a threat to the efforts of free nations to bring about world recovery and lasting peace.

Since the end of hostilities, the United States has invested its substance and its energy in a great constructive effort to restore peace, stability, and freedom to the world. . . .

Democracy alone can supply the vitalizing force to stir the peoples of the world into triumphant action, not only against their human oppression, but also against their ancient enemies—hunger, misery, and despair.

If we are to be successful in carrying out these policies, it is clear that we must have continued prosperity in this country and we must keep ourselves strong.

Slowly but surely we are weaving a world fabric of international security and growing prosperity.

We are aided by all who want relief from the lies of propaganda—who desire truth and sincerity.

We are aided by all who desire self-government and a voice in deciding their own affairs.

We are aided by all who long for economic security —for the security and abundance that men in free societies can enjoy.

We are aided by all who desire freedom of speech, freedom of religion, and freedom to live their own lives for useful ends. . . .

We are aided by all who wish to live in freedom from fear. . . .

I say to all men, what we have achieved in liberty, we will surpass in greater liberty.

Steadfast in our faith in the Almighty, we will advance toward a world where man's freedom is secure.

To that end we will devote our strength, our resources, and our firmness of resolve. With God's help, the future of mankind will be assured in a world of justice, harmony, and peace.

Freedom

As early as 1940, while a U.S. Senator , Truman raised the issue of civil rights:

Fear that Negro education may menace the white race's conception of racial safety displays nothing more than a narrow conception of good citizenship and an amazing ignorance of Negro characteristics. Always, it is the uneducated person, regardless of color, who is the dangerous citizen. It is the ignorant class among the people that is the criminal class. . . .

When we are honest enough to recognize each other's rights and are good enough to respect them, we will come to a more Christian settlement of our difficulties.

In the same address, Truman introduced a phrase from Booker T. Washington which he would later repeat often:

We must not forget that every community owes the

Negro a fair deal in regard to public utilities, lights, and sewers, street improvement, and water mains. We owe the Negro legal equality and a fair chance in the world for several reasons, not in the least of them because he is a human being and a natural-born American. Never must we forget that if we sink the Negro to the depth of hopeless degradation and make no provision for his comfort in housing or any other necessity of life, the law of compensation will take effect, and the whites, too, will go down with him.

As Booker T. Washington often said, "You cannot hold a Negro in the gutter unless some white man stays in the gutter to hold him there."

In his stirring address to the nation following the signing of the Japanese surrender in 1945, President Truman saw in the victory of war a lesson of liberty:

The thoughts and hopes of all America—indeed all the civilized world—are centered tonight on the battleship "Missouri." There on that small piece of American soil anchored in Tokyo Harbor, the Japanese have just officially laid down their arms. They have signed terms of unconditional surrender.

Four years ago, the thoughts and fears of the whole civilized world were centered on another piece of American soil—Pearl Harbor. The mighty threat to civilization which began there is now laid to rest. It was a long road to Tokyo—and a bloody one.

We shall not forget Pearl Harbor.

The Japanese militarists will not forget the USS "Missouri."

This is a victory of more than arms alone. This is a victory of liberty over tyranny. . . .

Back of it all (U.S. military power) was the will and spirit and determination of a free people—who know what freedom is, and who know that it is worth whatever price they had to pay to preserve it.

It was the spirit of liberty which gave us our armed strength and which made our men invincible in battle. We now know that the spirit of liberty, the freedom of the individual, and the personal dignity of man, are the strongest and toughest and most enduring forces in all the world.

Among Truman's most stirring addresses on the preservation of freedom is a speech delivered in 1949 at the World Memorial Park in Little Rock, Arkansas:
We are not a militaristic country. We do not glorify the military way of life. Some nations have taken greater pride in their military victories than in any other national achievements, but it has never been so with us. . . .

We entered the first World War to restore peace and to preserve human freedom; but when that war was finished, we turned aside from the task we had begun.

We turned our backs upon the League of Nations—the international organization which was established to maintain peace. We ignored the economic problems of the world, and adopted a tariff policy which only made them worse. We let our domestic affairs fall into the hands of selfish interests. . . .

This time we are fully aware of the mistakes that were made in the past. We are on guard against the indifference and isolationism which can only lead to the tragedy of war. This time we will not let our decisions be made for us by a little group of men who are concerned only with their own special interests. . . .

The goal we seek is a great one, and worth the price. Never has a nation had the opportunity which we have today to do so much for the peace and prosperity of mankind. Never has a nation had a better chance of reaching this high goal. . . .

We must not defeat our own efforts by doing only half the job that lies before us.

The brave men whose memory we honor here did all that was required of them. They did not fail us. We must not fail them in our efforts to reach the goal for which they died.

We must press on in the confidence that we will succeed in the mission a divine Providence has assigned to us.

In later years, Truman recalled that his most important decision while President was to enter the Korean

Conflict. During that conflict, in his State of the Union Address in 1952, Truman reminded Congress of America's objectives, drawing on George Washington's desperate struggle at Valley Forge:

To meet the crisis which now hangs over the world, we need many different kinds of strength: military, economic, political, and moral. And of all these, I am convinced that moral strength is the most vital.

When you come right down to it, it is the courage and the character of our Nation—and of each one of us as individuals—that will really decide how well we meet this challenge.

We are engaged in a great undertaking at home and abroad—the greatest, in fact, that any nation has ever been privileged to embark upon. We are working night and day to bring peace to the world and to spread the democratic ideals of justice and self-government to all people. Our accomplishments are already remarkable. We ought to be full of pride in what we are doing, and full of confidence and hope in the outcome. No nation ever had greater resources, or greater energy, or nobler traditions to inspire it.

And yet, day in and day out, we see a long procession of timid and fearful men who wring their hands and cry out that we have lost the way; that we don't know what we are doing; that we are bound to fail. Some say we should give up the struggle for peace, and others say we should have a war and get it over with. That is a terrible statement, but I have heard it. They want us to forget the great objective of preventing another world war—the objective for which our soldiers have been fighting in the hills of Korea.

If we are to be worthy of all that has been done for us by our soldiers in the field, we must be true to the ideals for which they are fighting. We must reject the counsels of defeat and despair. We must have the determination to complete the great work for which our men have laid down their lives.

In all we do we should remember who we are and what we stand for. We are Americans. Our forefathers had far greater obstacles than we have, and much poorer chances of success. They did not lose heart, or turn aside from their goals. In that darkest of all winters in American history, at Valley Forge, George Washington said: "We must not, in so great a contest, expect to meet with nothing but sunshine." With that spirit they won their fight for freedom.

We must have that same faith and vision. In the great contest in which we are engaged today we cannot expect to have fair weather all the way. But it is a contest just as important for this country and for all men as the desperate struggle that George Washington fought through to victory.

Let us prove, again, that we are not merely sunshine patriots and summer soldiers. Let us go forward, trusting in the God of Peace, to win the goals we seek.

Human Rights

Truman was the first President since Lincoln to make a national issue of civil rights. In a major policy address to Congress in 1948, he delivered these moving words on human dignity and civil rights:

The founders of the United States proclaimed to the world the American belief that all men are created equal, and that governments are instituted to secure the inalienable rights with which all men are endowed. . . .

These ideals inspired the peoples of other lands, and their practical fulfillment made the United States the hope of the oppressed everywhere. Throughout our history men and women of all colors and creeds, of all races and religions, have come to this country to escape tyranny and discrimination . . . with those who preceded them, they have helped to fashion and strengthen our American faith—a faith that can be simply stated:

We believe that all men are created equal and that they have the right to equal justice under law.

We believe that all men have the right to freedom

of thought and of expression and the right to worship as they please.

We believe that all men are entitled to equal opportunities for jobs, for homes, for good health, and for education.

We believe that all men should have a voice in their Government and that Government should protect, not usurp, the rights of the people.

We shall not, however, finally achieve the ideals for which this Nation was founded so long as any American suffers discrimination as a result of his race, or religion, or color, or the land of origin of his forefathers.

Unfortunately, there still are examples—flagrant examples—of discrimination which are utterly contrary to our ideals. Not all groups of our population are free from the fear of violence. Not all groups are free to live and work where they please or to improve their conditions of life by their own efforts. Not all groups enjoy the full privileges of citizenship and participation in the government under which they live.

We cannot be satisfied until all our people have equal opportunities for jobs, for homes, for education, for health, and for political expression, and until all our people have equal protection under the law. . . .

We know that our democracy is not perfect. But we do know that it offers a fuller, freer, happier life to our people than any totalitarian nation has ever offered.

*The President greets his 92-year-old mother upon
her arrival in Washington, D.C.*

Addressing the opening session of the United Nations Conference in San Francisco by radio from Washington.

Winston Churchill, President Truman, and Josef Stalin pause during the Potsdam Conference of 1945.

Outside the city of Berlin, the President reviews General Patton's Second Armored Division.

President Truman's famed early morning walk in his home town of Independence, Missouri.

Europeans in displaced persons camps. Truman proposed an immediate immigration measure to Congress which was not acted upon until 1948, and then in a discriminatory and inhumane manner, according to the President. He signed the controversial Displaced Persons Act in June, 1948, but immediately released the following statement:

This bill is flagrantly discriminatory. It mocks the American tradition of fair play. Unfortunately, it was not passed until the last day of the session. If I refused to sign this bill now, there would be no legislation on behalf of displaced persons until the next session of Congress. . . .

I have therefore signed the bill in the hope that its injustices will be rectified by the Congress at the first opportunity. . . .

Its good points can be stated all too briefly: At long last, the principle is recognized that displaced persons should be admitted to the United States. Two hundred thousand displaced persons may be admitted in the next 2 years, as well as 2,000 recent Czech refugees and 3,000 orphans.

The bad points of the bill are numerous. Together they form a pattern of discrimination and intolerance wholly inconsistent with the American sense of justice.

The bill discriminates in callous fashion against persons of Jewish faith. This brutal fact cannot be obscured by the maze of technicalities in the bill or by

Outside the city of Berlin, the President reviews General Patton's Second Armored Division.

President Truman's famed early morning walk in his home town of Independence, Missouri.

*In a familiar pose, the President speaks to the
nation over network radio.*

If we wish to inspire the people of the world whose freedom is in jeopardy, if we wish to restore hope to those who have already lost their civil liberties, if we wish to fulfill the promise that is ours, we must correct the remaining imperfections in our practice of democracy.

We know the way. We need only the will.

Truman reminisced about the decision he had made, early in 1947, to take a 'firm stand' on civil rights:

Back in 1947 a good many people advised me not to raise this whole question of civil rights. They said it would only make things worse. But you can't cure a moral problem or a social problem by ignoring it.

It is no service to the country to turn away from the hard problems—to ignore injustices and human suffering. It is simply not the American way of doing things. Of course, there are always a lot of people whose motto is "Don't rock the boat." They are so afraid of rocking the boat that they stop rowing. We can never get ahead that way.

If something is wrong, the thing to do is to dig it out, find out why it is wrong, and take sensible steps to put it right. We are all Americans together, and we can solve our hard problems together, including the problem of race relations.

At the close of World War II, there were 1.2 million

Europeans in displaced persons camps. Truman pro-
posed an immediate immigration measure to Con-
gress which was not acted upon until 1948, and then
in a discriminatory and inhumane manner, according
to the President. He signed the controversial Displaced
Persons Act in June, 1948, but immediately released
the following statement:

This bill is flagrantly discriminatory. It mocks the
American tradition of fair play. Unfortunately, it was
not passed until the last day of the session. If I refused
to sign this bill now, there would be no legislation on
behalf of displaced persons until the next session of
Congress....

I have therefore signed the bill in the hope that its
injustices will be rectified by the Congress at the first
opportunity....

Its good points can be stated all too briefly: At long
last, the principle is recognized that displaced persons
should be admitted to the United States. Two hundred
thousand displaced persons may be admitted in the
next 2 years, as well as 2,000 recent Czech refugees
and 3,000 orphans.

The bad points of the bill are numerous. Together
they form a pattern of discrimination and intolerance
wholly inconsistent with the American sense of justice.

The bill discriminates in callous fashion against persons of Jewish faith. This brutal fact cannot be obscured by the maze of technicalities in the bill or by

the protestations of some of its sponsors.

The primary device used to discriminate against Jewish displaced persons is the provision restricting eligibility to those displaced persons who entered Germany, Austria, or Italy on or before December 22, 1945. Most of the Jewish displaced persons who had entered Germany, Austria, or Italy by that time have already left; and most of the Jewish displaced persons now in those areas arrived there after December 22, 1945, and hence are denied a chance to come to the United States under this bill. By this device more than 90 per cent of the remaining Jewish displaced persons are definitely excluded. Even the eligible 10 per cent are beset by numerous additional restrictions written into the bill.

For all practical purposes, it must be frankly recognized, therefore, that this bill excludes Jewish displaced persons, rather than accepting a fair proportion of them along with other faiths.

The bill also excludes many displaced persons of the Catholic faith who deserve admission. Many anti-Communist refugees of Catholic faith fled into the American zones after December 22, 1945, in order to escape persecution in countries dominated by a Communist form of government. These too are barred by the December 22, 1945, dateline.

It is inexplicable, except upon the abhorrent ground of intolerance, that this date should have been chosen instead of April 21, 1947, the date on which General Clay closed the displaced persons camps to further admissions.

The Jewish and Catholic displaced persons . . . wrongly excluded by this bill, fled their native countries for the same basic reasons as Balts who came before December 22, 1945, and Czechs who came after January, 1948, who are rightly included. I sincerely hope that the Congress will remedy this gross discrimination at its earliest opportunity. . . .

I know what a bitter disappointment this bill is—to the many displaced victims of persecution who looked to the United States for hope; to the millions of our citizens who wanted to help them in the finest American spirit; to the many Members of Congress who fought hard but unsuccessfully for a decent displaced persons bill. I hope that this bitter disappointment will not turn to despair.

Faced with a Republican Congress, and balked by a conservative groundswell of public opinion in the late 1940s, Truman accomplished his two greatest acts in the field of civil rights not by legislation, but rather by executive order. In his capacity as the chief of the civil service, he issued an order on July 26, 1948, requiring that "All personnel actions taken by Federal appointing officers shall be based solely on merit and fitness; and such officers are authorized and directed

to take appropriate steps to insure that in all such ac-
tions there shall be no discrimination because of race,
color, religion, or national origin." On the same day,
by a single stroke of the pen, he began the desegrega-
tion of the armed services. This second order, an ex-
cerpt from which follows here, was issued in his capac-
ity as Commander-in-Chief of the Armed Forces:

It is essential that there be maintained in the armed
services of the United States the highest standards of
democracy, with equality of treatment and opportunity for all those who serve in our country's defense....

By virtue of the authority vested in me as President
of the United States, by the Constitution and the stat-
utes of the United States, and as Commander-in-Chief
of the armed services, it is hereby ordered as follows:
1. It is hereby declared to be the policy of the President
that there shall be equality of treatment and opportunity for all persons in the armed services without regard to race, color, religion or national origin. This
policy shall be put into effect as rapidly as possible,
having due regard to the time required to effectuate
any necessary changes without impairing efficiency or
morale.
2. There shall be created in the National Military Es-
tablishment an advisory committee to be known as
the President's Committee on Equality of Treatment
and Opportunity in the Armed Services, which shall
be composed of seven members to be designated by

the President.

3. The Committee is authorized on behalf of the President to examine into the rules, procedures and practices of the armed services in order to determine in what respect such rules, procedures and practices may be altered or improved with a view to carrying out the policy of this order. The Committee shall confer and advise with the Secretary of Defense, the Secretary of the Army, the Secretary of the Navy, and the Secretary of the Air Force, and shall make such recommendations to the President and to said Secretaries as in the judgment of the Committee will effectuate the policy hereof.

4. All executive departments and agencies of the Federal Government are authorized and directed to co-operate with the Committee in its work, and to furnish the Committee such information or the services of such persons as the Committee may require in the performance of its duties.

In his State of the Union address in 1949, Truman outlined the domestic programs and responsibilities of his administration:

During the last 16 years, our people have been creating a society which offers new opportunities for every man to enjoy his share of the good things of life. . . .

The Government must work with industry, labor, and the farmers in keeping our economy running at full speed. The Government must see that every American has a chance to obtain his fair share of our increasing abundance. These responsibilities go hand in hand.

We cannot maintain prosperity unless we have a fair distribution of opportunity and a widespread consumption of the products of our factories and farms.

Our Government has undertaken to meet these responsibilities. . . .

The Government has still other opportunities—to help raise the standard of living of our citizens. These opportunities lie in the fields of social security, health, education, housing, and civil rights. . . .

The fulfillment of this promise is among the highest purposes of government. The civil rights proposals I made to the 80th Congress, I now repeat to the 81st Congress. They should be enacted in order that the Federal Government may assume the leadership and discharge the obligations clearly placed upon it by the Constitution.

Throughout his long career, Truman maintained that democracy would triumph—and triumph without war—because men would ultimately come to believe in "the dignity of the individual":

Some people would have us believe that war is inevitable between the nations which are devoted to our concept of international organization and the concept which now bears the name of Communism. This is not the case. I am optimistic as I look toward the future, because I believe in the superior attraction for men's minds and hearts of the democratic principles which have been tried and tested in free nations, and which are now winning the allegiance of men throughout the world.

In the battle for men's minds our faith is more appealing, more dynamic, and stronger than any totalitarian force. The world longs for the kind of tolerance and mutual adjustment which is represented by democratic principles.

This country has had a revolutionary effect in the world since it was founded. Our democracy was born in a world of absolute monarchies. The idea which we made a living reality spread throughout the world and brought the day of the absolute monarch to an end. We have always been a challenge to tyranny of any kind. We are such a challenge today.

Our idea prevailed against the absolute monarchies of the nineteenth century. It is prevailing against the new and more terrible dictatorships of the twentieth century.

The reason is clear. Our idea of democracy speaks in terms which men can understand. It speaks of opportunity and tolerance and self-government. It speaks of the dignity of the individual, his freedom of conscience and the right to worship as he pleases. It does not exact blind loyalty to false ideas or improbable theories. It does not make a god out of the state, or out of man, or out of any human creation. . . .

Men want to live together in peace. They want to have useful work. They want to feel themselves united in brotherly affection. They want to enjoy that great privilege—a privilege denied to millions throughout the world today—the right to think their own thoughts and to have their own convictions.

These desires of mankind are satisfied by the democratic principles which we have put into practice. These principles are at work today as they were in the past. In the conflict that exists throughout the world, these are our greatest advantages. They should give us confidence that we shall eventually succeed in establishing the kind of international organization to preserve the peace for which men yearn. . . .

The peoples of the world look to the United States for the leadership of this great crusade for peace. We have not taken up this task lightly, and we will not lay it down.

We must go resolutely forward, step by step, toward the creation of a world in which we, and all people, can live and prosper in peace.

In 1951, Truman vetoed a bill that would have expanded the segregation of black Americans in the South by requiring Federal-aided schools to "conform to the laws of the individual states" in which they were located. On November 2, 1951, Truman explained his pocket veto of the bill in these words:

The basic purpose of this bill is meritorious. It would provide for the construction, maintenance, and operation of elementary and secondary schools in those localities where defense activities of the Federal Government have created unusual burdens. . . .

Unfortunately, however, the Congress has included one provision in this bill which I cannot approve. This provision would require a group of schools on Federal property which are now operating successfully on an integrated basis to be segregated. It would do so by requiring Federal schools on military bases and other Federal property to conform to the laws of the States in which such installations are located. . . .

This proposal, if enacted into law, would constitute a backward step in the efforts of the Federal Government to extend equal rights and opportunities to all our people. During the past few years, we have made rapid progress toward equal treatment and opportunity in those activities of the Federal Government where we have a direct responsibility to follow national rather than local interpretations of nondiscrimination. Two outstanding examples are the Federal civil service and our armed forces, where important advances have been made toward equalizing treatment and opportunity.

Not every school operated on a Federal reservation has been integrated. It is never our purpose to insist on integration without considering pertinent local factors; but it is the duty of the Federal Government to move forward in such locations and in such fields of activity as seem best and appropriate under individual conditions and circumstances.

We have assumed a role of world leadership in seeking to unite people of great cultural and racial diversity for the purpose of resisting aggression, protecting their mutual security and advancing their own economic and political development. We should not impair our moral position by enacting a law that requires a discrimination based on race. Step by step we are discarding old discriminations; we must not adopt new ones.

From his Commencement Day address at Howard University in 1952:

Our country is founded on the proposition that all men are created equal. This means that they should be equal before the law. They should enjoy equal political rights, and they should have equal opportunities for education, employment, and decent living conditions.

This is our belief, and we know it is right. We know it is morally right. And we have proved by experience that the more we practice that belief, the stronger, more vigorous, and happier our Nation becomes. . . .

This American Nation of ours is great because of its diversity—because it is a people drawn from many lands and many cultures, bound together by the ideals of human brotherhood. We must remember these things as we go forward in our efforts for world peace.

We should realize that much of the trouble in the world today is the result of false ideas of racial superiority. In the past the conduct of the democratic nations has too often been marred by a racial pride that has left its scars on the relations between East and West.

Today, as we reach a fuller understanding of the brotherhood of man, we are laying aside these old prejudices. We are working with the new nations of Asia and Africa as equals. Anything less would be a betrayal of the democratic ideals we profess. Better than any other country, the United States can reach out, through our diversity of races and origins, and deal as man to man with the different peoples of the globe.

In this way—in this spirit—we can help other peoples to build better lives for themselves. We can show that free peoples working together can change misery to happiness.

There are those who have said that this is America's century, but we want it to be more than that. We want it to be humanity's century.

The American Way

In a speech delivered in Chicago in 1949, Truman summed up his devout respect for The American Way in these words:

In this Nation, foreign policy is not made by the decisions of a few. It is the result of the democratic process, and represents the collective judgment of the people. Our foreign policy is founded upon an enlightened public opinion.

The importance of public opinion in the United States is not always understood or properly evaluated. Public opinion in a country such as ours cannot be ignored or manipulated to suit the occasion. It cannot be stampeded. Its formation is necessarily a slow process, because the people must be given ample opportunity to discuss the issues and reach a reasoned conclusion. But once a democratic decision is made, it represents the collective will of the Nation and can be depended upon to endure.

Those who rule by arbitrary power in other nations do not understand these things. For this reason, they do not realize the strength behind our foreign policy.

The major decisions in our foreign policy since the war have been made on the basis of an informed public opinion and overwhelming public support. . . .

Momentous decisions are the decisions not of the Government alone, but of the people of the United States. For this reason, it is clear that this country will steadfastly continue, together with other nations of like purpose, along the path we have chosen toward peace and freedom for the world.

The formation of foreign policy on the part of the democratic nations may be a slow and painful process, but the results endure.

In his veto of the Internal Security Act of 1950, President Truman charged the Congress with an insidious and un-American "frenzy" of Communist "witch-hunting." If this bill were to be made law, he said, "the next logical step would be to 'burn the books' ":

Until now, no one has suggested that we should abandon cultural and commercial relations with a country merely because it has a form of government different from ours. Yet [this bill] would require that.

As one instance, it is clear that under the definitions

of the bill the present government of Spain, among others, would be classified as "totalitarian." As a result, the Attorney General would be required to exclude from the United States all Spanish businessmen, students, and other nonofficial travelers who support the present government of their country. I cannot understand how the sponsors of this bill can think that such an action would contribute to our national security. . . .

[The bill] is so contrary to our national interests that it would actually put the Government into the business of thought control, by requiring the deportation of any alien who distributes or publishes, or who is affiliated with an organization which distributes or publishes, any written or printed matter advocating [or merely expressing belief in] the economic and governmental doctrines of any form of totalitarianism. . . .

Thus, the Attorney General would be required to deport any alien operating or connected with a well-stocked bookshop containing books on economics or politics written by supporters of the present government of Spain, of Yugoslavia, or any one of a number of other countries. . . .

There should be no room in our laws for such hysterical provisions. The next logical step would be to "burn the books."

From the same message to Congress Truman stated:

In a free country, we punish men for the crimes they commit, but never for the opinions they have. And the reason this is so fundamental to freedom is not, as many suppose, that it protects the few unorthodox from suppression by the majority. To permit freedom of expression is primarily for the benefit of the majority because it protects criticism, and criticism leads to progress. . . .

We need not fear the expression of ideas—we do need to fear their suppression.

On February 9, 1950, Senator Joseph R. McCarthy charged that the State Department was then employing 205 known Communists. He later reduced the number to 57, and still later to 10; an investigation disclosed that none were employed. But McCarthy had successfully turned the national concern about Communism into hysteria. During that era of slander, character assassination, and unproved accusations, one of the strongest voices of restraint was that of President Truman. He delivered his famous "Real Americanism" speech on August 15, 1951:

The keystone of our form of government is the liberty of the individual. The Bill of Rights, which protects our individual liberties, is the most fundamental part of our Constitution. . . .

Real Americanism means that we will protect freedom of speech—we will defend the right of people to say what they think, regardless of how much we may disagree with them.

Real Americanism means freedom of religion. It means that we will not discriminate against a man because of his religious faith.

Real Americanism means fair opportunities for all our citizens. It means that none of our citizens should be held back by unfair discrimination and prejudice.

Real Americanism means fair play. It means that a man who is accused of a crime shall be considered innocent until he has been proved guilty. It means that people are not to be penalized and persecuted for exercising their constitutional liberties.

Real Americanism means also that liberty is not license. There is no freedom to injure others. The Constitution does not protect free speech to the extent of permitting conspiracies to overthrow the Government. Neither does the right of free speech authorize slander or character assassination. . . .

[But real Americanism] is being undermined by some people in this country who are loudly proclaiming that they are its chief defenders. These people claim to be against Communism. But they are chipping away our basic freedoms just as insidiously and far more effectively than the Communists have ever been able to do.

These people have attacked the basic principle of fair play that underlies our Constitution. They are trying to create fear and suspicion among us by the use of slander, unproved accusations, and just plain lies.

They are filling the air with the most irresponsible kinds of accusations against other people. They are trying to get us to believe that our Government is riddled with Communism and corruption—when the fact is that we have the finest and most loyal body of civil servants in the world. These slandermongers are trying to get us so hysterical that no one will stand up to them for fear of being called a Communist.

Now, this is an old Communist trick in reverse. Everybody in Russia lives in terror of being called an anti-Communist. For once that charge is made against anybody in Russia—no matter what the facts are— he is on the way out.

In a dictatorship everybody lives in fear and terror of being denounced and slandered. Nobody dares stand up for his rights.

We must never let such a condition come to pass in this country.

Yet this is exactly what the scaremongers and hate-mongers are trying to bring about. Character assassination is their stock in trade. Guilt by association is their motto. They have created such a wave of fear and uncertainty that their attacks upon our liberties go almost unchallenged. Many people are growing frightened—and frightened people don't protest. . . .

Stop and think where this is leading us.

The growing practice of character assassination is already curbing free speech and it is threatening all our other freedoms. I daresay there are people here today who have reached the point where they are afraid to explore a new idea. How many of you are afraid to come right out in public and say what you think about a controversial issue? How many of you feel that you must "play it safe" in all things—and on all occasions?

I hope there are not many, but from all that I have seen and heard, I am afraid of what your answers might be.

For I know you have no way of telling when some unfounded accusation may be hurled at you, perhaps straight from the Halls of Congress.

Some of you have friends or neighbors who have been singled out for the pitiless publicity that follows accusations of this kind—accusations that are made without any regard for the actual guilt or innocence of the victim.

That is not playing fair. That is not Americanism. It is not the American way to slur the loyalty and besmirch the character of the innocent and the guilty alike. We have always considered it just as important to protect the innocent as it is to punish the guilty.

We want to protect the country against disloyalty— of course we do. We have been punishing people for disloyal acts, and we are going to keep on punishing the guilty whenever we have a case against them. But we don't want to destroy our whole system of justice in the process. We don't want to injure innocent people. And yet the scurrilous work of the scandalmongers gravely threatens the whole idea of protection for the innocent in our country today.

Perhaps the Americans who live outside of Washington are less aware of this than you and I. If that is so I want to warn them all. Slander, lies, character assassination—these things are a threat to every single citizen everywhere in this country. When even one American—who has done nothing wrong—is forced by fear to shut his mind and close his mouth, then all Americans are in peril.

It is the job of all of us—of every American who loves his country and his freedom—to rise up and put a stop to this terrible business.

Freedom is a precious heritage, and only fear, not Communism, could undermine it. Thus the President closed his eight years in office, stressing once again that the American way was founded in America's "faith" and "indomitable determination":

The Communists cannot deprive us of our liberties —fear can. The Communists cannot stamp out our faith in human dignity—fear can. Fear is an enemy within ourselves; and, if we do not root it out, it may destroy the very way of life we are so anxious to protect.

To beat back fear, we must hold fast to our heritage

as free men. We must renew our confidence in one another, our tolerance, our sense of being neighbors, fellow citizens. We must take our stand on the Bill of Rights. The inquisition, the star chamber, have no place in a free society.

Our ultimate strength lies not alone in arms, but in the sense of moral values and moral truths that give meaning and vitality to the purposes of free people. These values are our faith, our inspiration, the source of our strength, and our indomitable determination.

We face hard tasks, great dangers. But we are Americans and we have faced hardships and uncertainty before; we have adjusted before to changing circumstances. Our whole history has been a steady training for the work it is now ours to do.

No one can lose heart for the task, none can lose faith in our free ways, who stops to remember where we began, what we have sought, and what accomplished, all together as Americans.

I have lived a long time and seen much happen in our country. And I know, out of my own experience, that we can do what must be done.

When I think back to the country I grew up in—and then look at what our country has become—I am quite certain that having done so much, we can do more.

After all, it has been scarcely 15 years since most Americans rejected out-of-hand the wise counsel that aggressors must be "quarantined." The very concept of collective security, the foundation stone of all our actions now, was then strange doctrine, shunned and set aside. Talk about adapting; talk about adjusting; talk about responding as a people to the challenge of changed times and circumstances—there has never been a more spectacular example than this great change in America's outlook on the world.

Let all of us pause now, think back, consider carefully the meaning of our national experience. Let us draw comfort from it and faith and confidence in our future as Americans.

The Nation's business is never finished. The basic questions we have been dealing with, these eight years past, present themselves anew. That is the way of our society. Circumstances change and current questions take on different forms, new complications, year by year. But underneath, the great issues remain the same —prosperity, welfare, human rights, effective democracy, and above all, peace.

Now we turn to the inaugural of our new President. And in the great work he is called upon to do he will have need for the support of a united people, a confident people, with firm faith in one another and in our common cause. I pledge him my support as a citizen of our Republic, and I ask you to give him yours.

To him, to you, to all my fellow citizens, I say, Godspeed!

May God bless our country and our cause.

The Truman Wit

After his election to the presidency, Truman described his position to a group of freshmen Democrats of the House of Representatives:

There is one thing [I don't much like] about this job. It has no future to it. Every young man wants something to look forward to.

To a group of 4H members:

I hope to go back to the farm some day. Some people are in a hurry for me to go back, but I'm not going back as fast as they want me to.

President Truman was known for his pungent wit. He spoke directly, without mincing words. When he vetoed the Basing Point Bill of 1950 on the last day of the ten-day grace period, he was asked if it had been a difficult decision. Truman replied:

I intended to veto it all along. In fact, I feel like the blacksmith on the Missouri jury. The judge asked if he was prejudiced against the defendant. "Oh no, Judge," he said. "I think we ought to give him a fair trial. Then I think we ought to take the s.o.b. out and string him up."

After giving a speech about honesty to a group of Colgate University students, President Truman presented each one with a pen inscribed:

"I swiped this from Harry S. Truman."

When he interrupted a much-needed vacation in Florida to attend a dinner given by the Women's National Democratic Club, President Truman explained:

Mrs. Truman made this engagement for the two of us; and when I have a date with Mrs. Truman, I usually keep it.

Answering a question about the polls in 1948:

These polls are like sleeping pills designed to lull the voters into sleeping on election day. You might call them "sleeping polls."

The same doctor I told you about the other night in Pittsburgh—the Republican candidate—keeps handing out these sleeping polls, and some people have been taking them. This doctor keeps telling the people, "Don't worry, take a poll and go to sleep."

But most of the people are not being fooled.

From his veto of the Internal Security Act of 1950, which aimed to require all Communist organizations to register with the Attorney General and to furnish lists of their members:

The idea of requiring Communist organizations to divulge information about themselves is a simple and attractive one. But it is about as practical as requiring thieves to register with the sheriff.

In his address to the Democratic convention in 1948, Truman announced that he was calling the Republican-controlled 80th Congress back into a special mid-summer session "to get the laws the people need." It was a masterful stroke of pre-election political strategy, and Truman made the most of it to his colleagues in his convention address:

The Republican platform comes out for slum clearance and low-rental housing. I have been trying to get them to pass that housing bill ever since they met the first time, and it is still resting in the Rules Committee, that bill.

The Republican platform favors educational opportunity and promotion of education. I have been trying to get Congress to do something about that ever since they came there, and that bill is at rest in the House of Representatives.

The Republican platform is for extending and increasing social security benefits. Think of that! Increasing social security benefits! Yet when they had the opportunity, they took 750,000 off the social security rolls!

I wonder if they think they can fool the people of the United States with such poppycock as that!

There is a long list of these promises in that Republican platform. If it weren't so late, I would tell you all about them. I have discussed a number of these failures of the Republican 80th Congress. Every one of them is important. Two of them are of major concern to nearly every American family. They failed to do anything about high prices, they failed to do anything about housing.

My duty as President requires that I use every means within my power to get the laws the people need on matters of such importance and urgency.

I am therefore calling this Congress back into session July 26th.

On the 26th day of July, which out in Missouri we call "Turnip Day," I am going to call Congress back and ask them to pass laws to halt rising prices, to meet the housing crisis—which they are saying they are for in their platform.

At the same time I shall ask them to act upon other

vitally needed measures such as aid to education, which they say they are for; a national health program; civil rights legislation, which they say they are for; and an increase in the minimum wage, which I doubt very much they are for.

Reminiscing about Stalin:

I invited Stalin to come to Washington, and he said, "God willing, I will come." Well, I haven't met anybody yet who believes me, but that is what he said to me.

Truman delivered his famous "Doctor Dewey" parable many times during the campaign:

My opponent is conducting a very peculiar campaign. He has set himself up as a kind of doctor with a magic cure for all the ills of mankind.

Let's imagine that we, the American people, are going to see this doctor. It's just our usual routine checkup which we have every four years.

We go into the doctor's office.

"Doctor," we say, "we're feeling fine."

"Is that so?" asks the doctor. "You been bothered much by issues lately?"

"Not bothered, exactly," we say. "Of course, we've had quite a few. We've had the issues of high prices, and housing, education and social security, and a few others."

"That's bad," says the doctor. "You shouldn't have so many issues."

"Is that right?" we say. "We thought that issues were a sign of political health."

"Not at all," says the doctor. "You shouldn't think about issues. What you need is my brand of soothing syrup—I call it 'unity.' "

Then the doctor edges up a little closer.

"Say, you don't look so good," he says.

We say to him, "Well, that seems strange to me, Doc. I never felt stronger, never had more money, and never had a brighter future. What is wrong with me?"

Well, the doctor looks blank, and says, "I never discuss issues with a patient. But what you need is a major operation."

"Will it be serious, Doc?" we say.

"No, not very serious," he says. "It will just mean taking out the complete works and putting in a Republican Administration."

That's the kind of campaign you're getting from the Republicans. They won't talk about the issues, but they insist that a major operation is necessary.

Truman took his office seriously, but not himself. Once when the Presidential motorcade was late arriving at his home in Independence, Missouri, from nearby Kansas City Metropolitan Airport, the President of the United States explained:

We were stopped by a police car, and had to pull over. Seems there were some very important people going through town.

In his remarks to new Congressmen in 1949, Truman told this story:

There was an old county judge who was with me on the county court in Jackson County (Missouri) . . . and he gave me some advice before I left Independence to come to Washington.

He said, "Harry, don't you go to the Senate with an inferiority complex. You sit there about six months, and you wonder how you got there. But after that, you wonder how the rest of them got there."

On the subject of war:

Wars are different from baseball games, where, at the end of the game, the teams get dressed and leave the park.

The phrase "Give 'em hell, Harry" became the battle cry of Truman's presidential campaign in 1948. He later explained that someone had shouted it at him from the crowd at a rally in Seattle:

I told him at that time, and I have been repeating it ever since, that I have never deliberately given anybody hell. I just tell the truth on the opposition—and they think it's hell.

Commenting on the difference between a Republican political leader and a Democratic political leader:

When a leader is in the Democratic Party he's a boss. When he's in the Republican Party he's nothing but a leader. But there's no difference in them.

At President Truman's press conferences, reporters often got more than they bargained for:

Q: Mr. President, this morning's [Washington] Post has an editorial saying it thinks you ought to appoint a lot of Republicans. . . .

A: I'm a Democrat.

Q: Mr. President, the New York Times this morning has a story out of Paris saying that there is—may be— a drastic change in our foreign policy. . . .

A: I haven't heard about it, and I make the policy.

Q: Mr. President, have you seen any flying saucers?

A: Only in the newspapers. And you know what I think about the newspapers.

Describing the Republicans in the campaign:

Herbert Hoover once ran on the slogan, "Two cars in every garage." Apparently the Republican candidate this year is running on the slogan, "Two families in every garage". . . . This year the same [Republican] candidate is back with us, and he is saying much the same thing: that he likes our Democratic laws, but that he can run them much better than we can.

It sounds like the same old phonograph record; but this year the record has a crack, and the needle gets stuck in it. The crack was provided by the Republican Eightieth Congress.

In 1948, every time the candidate says, "I can do it better," the crack says, "We're against it."

Relaxing with friends in Caruthersville, Missouri, President Truman was asked to play Paderewski's Minuet. He sat down at the piano, chuckled, and announced:

When Stalin heard me play this [at Potsdam], he signed the protocol.

After Truman was nominated for the Vice-Presidency in 1944, his cousin, General Ralph E. Truman, remarked to the nominee's mother that she must be very proud of her son. She answered with a smile:

Oh, well, I liked him just as well before.

During Truman's "whistle-stop" campaign of 1948, he was speaking from the back platform of a train in Barstow, California, when a woman shouted: "You sound like you have a cold!" Truman shot back:

That's because I ride around in the wind with my mouth open.

Set at The Castle Press
in Trump Medieval,
a Venetian face designed
by Georg Trump, Munich.

Printed on Hallmark
Eggshell Book paper.
Designed by
Harald Peter.